Flies for Dinner

Written by Robert Collins

What eats flies

for dinner?

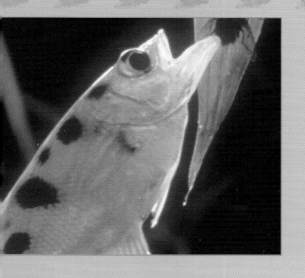

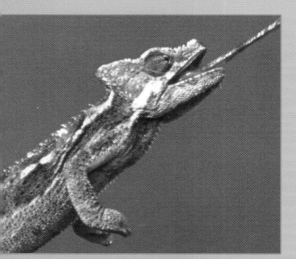

This fish eats flies

for dinner.

Archerfish

5

This spider eats flies

for dinner.

Garden Spider

This bird eats flies

for dinner.

Black-Backed Wren

This lizard eats flies for dinner.

Bearded Chameleon

This plant eats flies, too!

Look out, fly!

Venus Flytrap